BEGINNER'S GOLF
for KIDS
ages 6-106

By
Don Emerick,
Ken Kebow,
and Jim Fisher

Illustrated by Dean Baldridge

Quality Sports Publications

ISBN 1-885758-12-X

Cover design by Mick McCay

Illustrations by Dean Baldridge
Photos courtesy of the authors

For information write or FAX:
Quality Sports Publications
24 Buysse Drive
Coal Valley, IL 61240
(800) 464-1116 • (309) 234-5016 • (309) 234-5019 FAX

Duane Brown, Project Director
Melinda Brown, Designer

Printed in the U.S.A.

Publisher's Cataloging-in-Publication
Tiger's tips : beginner's golf for kids 6 - 106 / By Don
    Emerick, Ken Kebow, Dean Baldridge and Jim Fisher ;
    Dean Baldridge, illustrator. -- 1st ed.
    p. cm.
    Includes index.
    ISBN: 1-885758-12-X

1. Golf for children.   I. Emerick, Donald J.
GV966.3.T54 1998   796.352'0834
                           QBI98-881

**Dedicated to the heart
of the game
– the kid in all of us.**

Table of Contents

Acknowledgements

This book is dedicated to:
Chuck and Marjorie Baldridge for always
supporting my creative ideas;
and to my wife Sally for encouraging me to
follow through with my dreams;
and to my twin daughters, Marcie and Jodi,
for the smile on their face everyday
that puts a smile on my face.

– Dean Baldridge

My parents Alex and Olga Emerick
for always encouraging me in golf
from my time in Jr. Golf to fulfilling my dream
of becoming a PGA Professional;
and to my wife Terrie and daughter Kelsie
for sharing my love of golf and accepting it
as part of our lives; and to my brother David,
a fellow PGA Golf Professional who I played
many rounds of golf with since we were
10 years old.

– Don Emerick

My parents Duke and Sheila Kebow
for always believing in me and
encouraging my creative ventures;
To my wonderful wife and friend Tina,
I love you with all my heart
(thanks for your patience with my "projects!")
and to three wonderful children,
Amber, Landon and Dylan (Tiny) - you guys
make me happy and keep me smiling!

– *Ken Kebow*

I would like to thank my mom and dad,
June and Bob Fisher, for giving me the opportunity
to enjoy and eventually make my career in golf;
to my wife Debra, thanks for your
unconditional love and support;
to my kids Jessica and Max, I hope I can
offer you the same opportunities that
were given to me;
and lastly to Don, Dean and Ken,
thank you for including me and
realizing we all share the same passion.

– *Jim Fisher*

Golf is a game to have FUN!

Introduction

Welcome to the wonderful game of golf!

Whether someone is six years old or 106 years old, golf is a game any person can enjoy their entire lifetime. You are never too young to learn the game of golf and you are never too old to have fun playing it. You can play alone or enjoy a round of golf with friends or family members.

Golf is unique in many ways. A person does not need to be extremely strong or have special athletic abilities to play golf. The skill level of a golfer is not important since beginners, as well as professionals, can enjoy this exciting game. And golfers come in all shapes, sizes and ages.

It is believed that almost 900 years ago Roman shepherds would pass the time watching their flocks of sheep by hitting stones with curved sticks. This was perhaps the first game of golf! Many years later in the 1700's, people in Scotland, a country in Europe, hit feather-stuffed balls with pieces of hickory wood. A game much like our modern game of golf was even played in America's original 13 colonies. And in 1893 a man named Charles MacDonald built the first 18 hole golf course in the United States.

Your interest in golf may have come from playing miniature golf with your friends. Or perhaps you got excited about the game watching a young professional golfer win a major golf tournament on television. No matter how you became interested in golf or how much you have already played, *Tiger's Tips* will help you improve your golf and increase your enjoyment of the game.

The first chapter in *Tiger's Tips* will take a look at **Golf Terms."** In this chapter the meaning of each term will be explained in detail. We'll explain terms that have to do with golf clubs, golf holes, types of shots and many others. Understanding the words and terms used in any sport is a big step towards a better understanding of the sport itself.

Chapter Two in *Tiger's Tips* will examine **"Clubs, Scorecards and Golf Holes."** This chapter is a "diagram & drawing" chapter. We will diagram the elements that make up a golf club and explain what each part of the club is responsible for. We also will provide a drawing of a typical "golf hole" and cover the different elements that make up a hole of golf (teeing area, fairway, rough, hazard, green, etc.). This chapter also will diagram and explain a golf scorecard.

Chapter Three in *Tiger's Tips* will explain **"How The Golf Club Works."** The chapter outlines why each club hits the way it does. We'll talk about woods, long irons, mid-irons, short irons, sand wedge and the putter. And at the end of the chapter, you will help Tiger choose the right club on the course and help Tiger make par on a golf hole!

Tiger's Tips' **"Getting Started"** covers the information you need as a beginning golfer. Utilizing a number of cartoons and photographs, Chapter Four will cover topics such as Junior Golf programs, beginning swing clinics, what you need when you venture to the course, dress code, what type of course a beginning player should play and warming up prior to your tee time. One goal of this chapter will be to explain to beginning players that there is no hurry to play golf on an actual course. Time spent with beginning lessons and swing clinics, as well as practice time on the driving range, can make a beginning golfer's first adventure onto a real course much more enjoyable and exciting.

The next chapter in *Tiger's Tips* will cover **"The Golf Swing."** Understanding the fundamentals of the swing is the key to a successful golf swing. Chapter Five, using a series of photos and cartoons, will cover swing fundamentals and provide a number of tips that can help a young golfer develop a strong swing. Chapter Five will conclude with a "troubleshooting" section with our cartoon

Tiger explaining how certain problems with a incorrectly hit golf ball can be fixed with a slight adjustment to one's golf swing.

"Golf Rules & Safety," *Tiger's Tips* Chapter Six, will cover the basic rules of the game, as well as provide an overview of safety issues in regards to golf. "Golf Rules" covers how to count one's strokes, penalty strokes and much more. "Golf Safety" will cover safety issues in regards to those people you are playing golf with, as well as others on the course. Specific topics will include safe swinging of a golf club, how to warn other players of a ball you have hit in their direction (FORE), how to protect oneself from balls other may have hit, etc. This chapter also will explain how losing one's temper and ever throwing a golf club is not allowed and bad sportsmanship.

"Golf Etiquette" (manners) is an extremely important part of the game of golf. *Tiger's Tips* Chapter Seven will cover all areas of golf etiquette including information about doing one's part to keep the golf course in top condition (divot replacement, fixing one's ball mark on the green, etc.) as well as common courtesy etiquette in regards to other players (who hits first in a group, being courteous to other groups playing on the course, etc.). Also, special attention will be paid to one's etiquette on the greens of a course. Cartoons featuring Tiger and photographs of young golfers will help us explain the finer points of golf etiquette in an effective and entertaining manner.

TIGER SAYS At certain points throughout the book, a small Tiger, like the one next to this paragraph, will appear to draw attention to a particularly special and helpful tip. When this Tiger appears pay special attention to the bold words next to Tiger. These tips are especially helpful and important.

There is no other sport in the world like golf. Boy or girl, young or old, tall or short, golf is a game that can be enjoyed by anyone. While some players enjoy competing against other golfers, most people play the game simply for fun. They play with family, friends or with people they have just met at the course. Golf is also an outdoor game often played near trees, fields, lakes, streams and even by the ocean. And golf is one sport where you don't need a whole team to play. You can play with anywhere from one to three other players or you can play by yourself. And you can practice alone and always improve your game, no matter how long you've been golfing.

And a note to the parents of aspiring golfers.

Getting your children involved in the game of golf is a great activity the entire family can enjoy. Since golf can be played at any age, golf is an activity that you and your children will enjoy together for many years. Golf teaches good sportsmanship, honesty and individual competition, as a golfer is always trying to improve their own game. Read through and enjoy this book with your young golfer. It could be the beginning of many years spent together enjoying the game of golf.

And to the young golfer . . . welcome to *Tiger's Tips*!

CHAPTER 1
GOLF TERMS

Every sport has its own "language." And golf is no exception! The words and terms used in the game of golf are different than other sports and may be words that are only used when talking about golf.

This chapter will cover many of the words and terms used in the game of golf. These words and terms are used on the course while playing golf and it is important for all golfers to understand what is being said about the game while they are playing. Don't worry about memorizing these words. As you play more and more golf, you will better understand what each word and term means.

The words we explain in this chapter will appear again and again in this book. When a word is used in the following chapters and you have trouble remembering what it means, you can always come back to this chapter (pages 16-24), each time you need to better understand the golf terms that appear in *Tiger's Tips*.

GOLF TERMS
(in alphabetical order)

Ace - when a golfer hits their first shot of a hole into the cup, also called a "Hole in One"

AJGA - American Junior Golf Association

Alignment - the lining up of your body to your ball and the target

"Away" - ball resting farthest away from the hole, making it "away" and to be played next

Backspin - backwards spinning of the ball caused by the loft of each golf club - backspin stops the ball from rolling after landing

Backswing - the movement of the golf club away from the ball to get the club set in position for the downswing

Ball Mark - the hole the ball makes when it lands on the green

Ball Position - location of the ball in your stance relative to the position of your feet

Ball Washer - a device used to clean golf balls and usually found in the teeing area of each hole

Birdie - the name for a score one below the par of a hole

Bite - a term used when you are hoping your ball stops as soon as it hits the ground or green

Bogey - the name for a score one above the par of a hole

Break - a term used to define which way your ball will roll on the green or which direction it will "break" when stroked

Bunker - an area prepared and filled with sand and strategically placed on a golf hole to add challenge to the game; also called a sand trap

Casual Water - when water is visible under your feet and not in a water hazard, this allows you a free drop

Chili Dip - hitting the ground before the ball resulting in a miss hit

Chip and Run - a low shot with a lot of roll used when your ball is close to the green.

Chip Shot - a shot that is hit to the green with a lower loft club that travels low and a short distance in the air before reaching the green and rolling into position

Clubhead - the part of the club that comes in contact with the ball when you swing

Clubhouse - the building where you will find the golf shop, the lunch room and restrooms on a golf course

Cup - the hole on the green into which the golf ball is hit - The cup measures 4-1/2 inches across (diameter) and 4 inches deep

Dimple - the pattern on the outside cover of a golf ball

Divot - a piece of turf (grass and dirt) removed from the ground by the club as it strikes the ball

Dogleg - the design of a hole that curves to the right or left as the hole is played

Double Bogey - the name for a score two above the par of a hole

Downswing - the forward movement of swinging the club after the backswing with the intent to hit the ball

Draw - A golf shot that is made to curve slightly to the left

Driver - the club used for maximum distance - usually hit off the tee, as a longer hole's first shot

Driving Range - the area where golf is taught and practiced - the range is usually divided into swing stations for each individual

Drop - while incurring a penalty you must drop a new ball in play if your ball is lost or unplayable

Eagle - the name for a score two below the par of a hole

Executive Course - a golf course with shorter holes and generally par 3 and par 4 holes

Face - the part of the clubhead that actually hits the ball

Fade - a ball that is meant to curve slightly to the right

Fairway - the closely cut grass that is used on the main playing area that stretches from the tee to the green on each hole

Flagstick - the pole (usually with a flag and the hole number on it) that is on the green and shows the position of the hole - also called the pin

Flex - the bending of a shaft during the swing

"Fore" - a word used to alert other golfers about a golf ball heading in their direction

Foursome - a group of four players

Fringe - the first 2-3 feet of grass surrounding the green usually cut a little longer than the grass on the putting green

Golf Course - 18 holes of golf that are laid out over a specific area and numbered consecutively - some golf courses may have only 9 holes

Golf Shop - the building at a golf course where a golfer checks in for their tee time, pays their green fees and purchases golf equipment, and sometimes food and drink

Green - the closely mown area of grass surrounding each of the holes to be used for putting

Green Fee - the sum of money paid to play a round of golf and usually collected at the golf shop

Grip - the way one holds onto a golf club - the three different types of grips are the Interlock, the Overlap and the Ten-Finger grip

Ground Under Repair - usually outlined by paint, an area that is considered unplayable resulting in a free drop

Handicap - strokes given to a player based on the average of scores turned in, allowing players of different ability the chance to compete with each other

Hazard - any unprepared or difficult obstacle on any given golf hole

Heel - the part of the club that joins the shaft to the clubhead

Hole In One - when a golfer hits their first shot of a hole into the cup, also known as an "Ace"

Honor - the first player to hit the ball off the tee because his or her score was the lowest on the previous hole

Hook - a shot that travels with a big curve to the left of your target usually caused by an inside-out swing path at the ball

Iron - a golf club with a tilted metal head that hits the ball high in the air so it lands with little roll

LPGA - Ladies Professional Golfers Association

Lip - the sharp edge on the hole (cup)

Loft - the amount of tilt between the top and bottom of the clubhead - a club's loft determines how high and far your shot will travel

Marshal - the golf course worker in charge of keeping the pace of play moving to avoid slow play on the course

Out of Bounds - the area outside the golf course where a golfer cannot play their ball - out of bounds is usually marked by white stakes

PGA - Professional Golfers Association of America

Par - the score an expert golfer should have on a hole - par scores are determined by the yardage of the hole

Par 3 - the score an expert golfer should have on a hole up to 245 yards long

Par 4 - the score an expert golfer should have on a hole from 245 to 475 yards long

Par 5 - the score an expert golfer should have on a hole 475 yards long and up

Penalty Stroke - a stroke that is added to a player's score when that player has broken a rule - for example hitting the ball into a water hazard would result in a penalty stroke added to that hole's score

Pitching Wedge - a iron with a great deal of loft that is used for high, short shots

Pitch-N-Putt - a golf course usually made up of par 3 holes with distances of 100 yards or less

Pitch Shot - a short distance shot (10 - 50 yards) that is hit high in the air with a higher lofted club to the putting green - the shot generally has little to no roll when it lands

Provisional Ball - an additional ball that is played on a hole when a golfer's original ball may be lost or unplayable

Putt - the stroke used to roll the ball while on the green

Putter - the golf club used to roll a putt on the green

Rough - tall grass or roughage that is on either side of the fairway and usually cut higher than the grass in the fairway

Round - a complete game of 18 holes of golf

Rub of the Green - the name given for a bad bounce or unfortunate happening to the golf ball due to an outside source

Sand Wedge - a club with a lot of loft and a heavier bottom specially designed to hit balls out of bunkers

Scorecard - used by the golfer to keep track of their strokes on each hole - a scorecard has information about each golf hole including the distance of the hole and the par, as well as, specific rules for that golf course.

Slice - a shot that travels with a curve to the right of your target and usually caused by an outside-in swing path at the ball

Stance - the positioning of your feet and body up to the ball

Tee - a wooden or plastic peg that the ball rests on for your tee shot on each hole

Tee Box - the marked area where a golfer hits their first shot of each golf hole

Teeing Ground - the area of grass mown to a short height where the start of each hole is defined by "tee markers"

Toe - the part of the clubhead that is farthest from the shaft

USGA - United States Golf Association

Unplayable Lie - when a golf ball rests in a position considered not playable

Whiff - when a golfer swings and completely misses the ball - a whiff counts as one stroke

Wood - the club with the largest hitting surface and often used for long distance shots

Yardage Markers - objects positioned on a golf hole to help indicate the distance from that place on the golf hole, to the center of the green

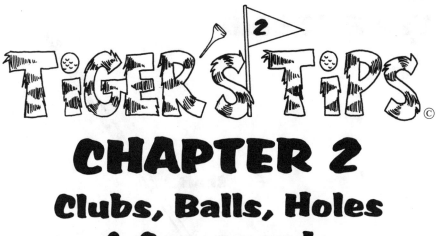

CHAPTER 2
Clubs, Balls, Holes & Scorecards

Here's how the game works:

- You swing the golf club at the ball.

- The object is to get the ball into the cup in the least amount of strokes as possible.

- The number of strokes it takes to get the golf ball into the cup goes onto your golf scorecard.

- You do this for an entire round of golf and you have a lot of fun while doing it!

The Golf Club

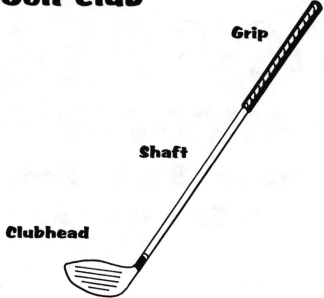

GOLF CLUBS are basically made up of three separate parts - the grip, the shaft and the clubhead.

- The **GRIP** is the handle of the club.

- The **SHAFT** connects the handle to the clubhead.

- The **CLUBHEAD** is the part of the club that comes in contact with the ball.

A Clubhead

A clubhead has a **HEEL**, a **FACE** and a **TOE**.

- The **HEEL** of the clubhead is the part of the club that joins the shaft to the clubhead.

- The **FACE** of the clubhead is the actual surface that hits the golf ball.

- The **TOE** of the clubhead is the part farthest from the shaft.

A set of golf clubs has **WOODS, IRONS** and a **PUTTER**.

- A **WOOD** is the club that is designed to hit a golf ball far and straight. Woods are the longest clubs in your golf bags. Many years ago clubs were actually made out of wood and that's why they called them woods. Now most of the golf clubs, including the woods, are made out of steel. Woods can be numbered from 1 to 9.

TIGER SAYS

Most golfers should carry a #1 wood, a #3 wood and a #5 wood in their golf bag. Beginners need only a #3 and a #5 wood.

- **IRONS** are used as you get closer to the golf hole. An iron will hit the ball high into the air so it will not roll far from the hole when it lands. Long Irons are irons #1, #2, #3 and #4, Middle Irons are #5, #6 and #7 and the Short Irons are #8, #9 and a Pitching Wedge.

The last of the irons is the Sand Wedge. This club is specifically designed to get the golf ball out of the sand trap or bunker. The heavier bottom, or sole of the club, makes the ball get up in the air easier than the other clubs. This makes it the ideal club to hit the golf ball out of the bunkers and onto the green.

- Once your ball is on the fringe or on the green, you will use a **PUTTER** to roll the ball into the cup. The putter does not lift a ball into the air at all, but rather rolls it along the putting surface into the hole.

TIGER SAYS

Here is a simple rule to remember about golf clubs - the longer the club the further the shot will travel.

Also, the shorter the club the shorter the shot will travel.

Now you know what each club's purpose is. Later in Chapter Five, we will explain why each club hits the way we have described in this chapter.

THE GOLF BALL

A golf ball weighs 1.62 ounces and is 1.68 inches across (diameter). Golf balls can be constructed in a solid-piece, a two-piece, a three-piece or a four-piece form.

- A solid-piece golf ball is recommended for the beginning golfer. These balls are very tough and also are commonly used on the driving range.

- The two-piece golf ball is simply a solid center surrounded by a hard plastic cover. The two-piece ball is tough like the solid-piece ball but gives a golfer more control and better distance.

- The three-piece ball and four-piece ball have a small rubber ball with rubber bands wrapped tightly around it. The outside cover of the ball is a rubber material called balata, which is the dried sap from a West Indian tree. A synthetic, or manufactured, version of balata is also used on the three-piece ball. Professionals and very serious golfers use these balls because they can control their flight better than the other balls. But they are not as tough as the balls described above and may get damaged more easily in a game of golf.

TIGER SAYS

At this stage of the game save your money and use the solid-piece "tough" balls . . . unless your mom or dad will pay for the good balls!

The dimple patterns stamped onto the outside cover of a golf ball help control the flight of the ball. The size and pattern of the dimples are different from ball to ball. The general rule is the more dimples on the golf ball the lower and straighter the ball will fly.

THE GOLF HOLE

The object of golf is to hit the ball until it reaches the small opening in the ground known as the cup. The cup measures 4-1/2 inches across (diameter) and 4 inches deep.

Most golf courses have 9 or 18 holes. Playing 18 holes of golf is considered a round. It is called this because many early golf courses in Scotland were laid out in a circle, meaning you began and finished much in the same area.

A Golf Hole

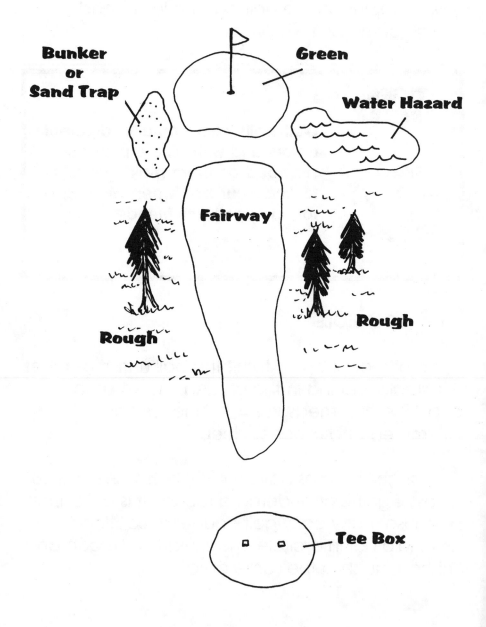

Bunker or Sand Trap

Green

Water Hazard

Fairway

Rough

Rough

Tee Box

Each golf hole is made up of five elements:

THE TEE BOX
THE FAIRWAY
THE ROUGH
THE HAZARDS (not all holes)
THE GREEN

- The **TEE BOX** is the area set up by two markers from which you hit your first shot, or tee shot, of each hole. Your ball must be hit from between these two markers. Many golf courses will have three sets of markers in each tee box.

TIGER SAYS Beginning and less experienced golfers should hit from between the two red markers. As you get better, you can move back and hit from the white tee markers and then from the blue tee markers.

You may hit your first shot of each hole off a two inch wooden peg called a tee. This is the only time you can use a tee. All other shots of the hole must be hit off the ground until you "tee up" again.

- The **FAIRWAY** is the short green grass that runs from the tee box to the green of each golf hole. The grass on the fairway is cut to a height of 1 to 2 inches and a golfer should try their best to keep their ball in the fairway all the way from the tee box to the green on each hole.

One of the challenges of golf is keeping your ball on the fairway and out of the ROUGH on the way to the green.

- The **ROUGH** is a tougher area to hit your ball out of. Often the grass is 3 to 6 inches high in the rough (it can be hard just to find your ball!) and the rough also can contain bushes and trees. Don't worry . . . you'll recognize the rough soon enough!

- **OUT OF BOUNDS** may look like the rest of the rough surrounding the fairway. However these out of bounds areas are usually marked with a sign or a white stake. A golfer cannot play their ball from these out of bounds areas. There is a penalty stroke for a player who hits their ball out of bounds. More of these rules will be covered in Chapter Six.

- A golf hole can have many types of **Water Hazards**. Ponds, streams and lakes are all considered hazards on a golf hole. A golfer who hits into these areas often will lose a ball and be penalized a stroke as well.

- **BUNKERS** (sand traps) also are considered hazards on a golf course. While there is not a penalty stroke for hitting into a bunker, it is often challenging for a golfer to successfully hit out of one of these hazards.

- The **GREEN** is the area where the golfer ultimately hits his ball into the cup. The grass on the green is cut shorter than the grass on the fairway. A six foot removable pole with a flag on the end sits in the cup, identifying it for the golfers as they hit towards the green. This pole is called the flagstick, or the pin, and is removed from the cup once the golfers' balls are on the green.

When you play a golf hole you count the number of times you hit your ball from the tee box until you sink it into the cup on the green. This total, plus any penalty strokes from hazards or out of bounds areas, will be your final score for that golf hole.

THE GOLF SCORECARD

The following two pages show a golf scorecard and explains how it works and how to use it. It is very important to count all your strokes to make sure your score is accurate.

A Golf Scorecard

Tips about filling out the card: bolded type
Information about the card: unbolded type

Length (yards) for each hole. Each colored tee is a different length to make the holes more difficult.

The set of tees you play from is determined by your ability.

Names of players

Players scores for each hole

The par for each hole

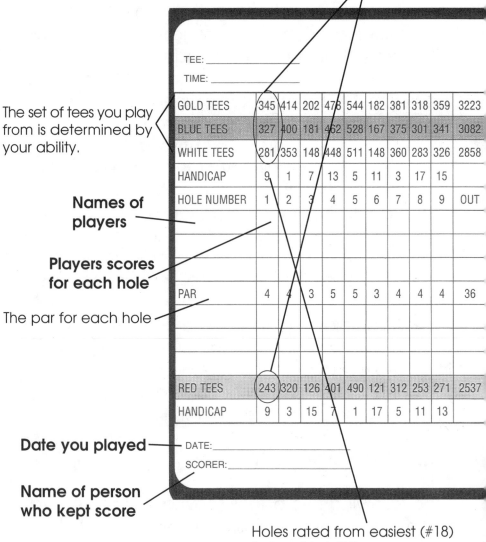

TEE:										
TIME:										
GOLD TEES	345	414	202	478	544	182	381	318	359	3223
BLUE TEES	327	400	181	462	528	167	375	301	341	3082
WHITE TEES	281	353	148	448	511	148	360	283	326	2858
HANDICAP	9	1	7	13	5	11	3	17	15	
HOLE NUMBER	1	2	3	4	5	6	7	8	9	OUT
PAR	4	4	3	5	5	3	4	4	4	36
RED TEES	243	320	126	401	490	121	312	253	271	2537
HANDICAP	9	3	15	7	1	17	5	11	13	

DATE: _____

SCORER: _____

Date you played — DATE:

Name of person who kept score — SCORER:

Holes rated from easiest (#18) to toughest (#1)

36

Score an expert golfer would expect to shoot from each of these tees.

Slope rating adjusts peoples handicaps, depending on the difficulty of the golf course.

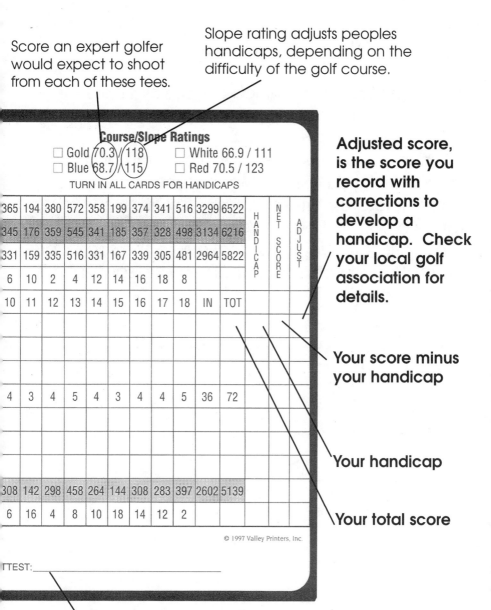

Course/Slope Ratings
☐ Gold 70.3 / 118   ☐ White 66.9 / 111
☐ Blue 68.7 / 115   ☐ Red 70.5 / 123
TURN IN ALL CARDS FOR HANDICAPS

365	194	380	572	358	199	374	341	516	3299	6522	H A N D I C A P	N E T S C O R E	A D J U S T			
345	176	359	545	341	185	357	328	498	3134	6216						
331	159	335	516	331	167	339	305	481	2964	5822						
6	10	2	4	12	14	16	18	8								
10	11	12	13	14	15	16	17	18	IN	TOT						
4	3	4	5	4	3	4	4	5	36	72						
308	142	298	458	264	144	308	283	397	2602	5139						
6	16	4	8	10	18	14	12	2								

© 1997 Valley Printers, Inc.

TTEST: _____

Adjusted score, is the score you record with corrections to develop a handicap. Check your local golf association for details.

Your score minus your handicap

Your handicap

Your total score

You must sign your name showing you agree with the scores on the card.

On the back of your scorecard you will usually find:

- A **MAP** of the golf course.

- **LOCAL RULES** which are special rules for the golf course you are playing.

When you sign your scorecard at the end of your round, you are stating that the scores on each hole are correct. Each player is responsible for his or her score on every hole. When you sign the scorecard, you must make sure the scores are correct or you can be penalized or disqualified if you are playing in an event.

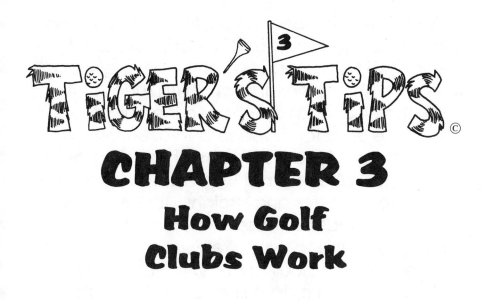

CHAPTER 3
How Golf Clubs Work

It is very important in any sport to be familiar with and understand your equipment. Golf is no different. A clear understanding of what each golf club is able to do and a knowledge of what club to use in any golfing situation will put you on track to being a better golfer.

Each golf club in your bag is designed to hit the ball in a certain way and has been created for specific hitting situations on the golf course. As we mentioned in the previous chapters, the woods are most often used to hit the ball when you are far from the green and irons are most often used to hit shots when you are closer to the green. The design of each club helps accomplish these goals. Let's look at why clubs hit the way they do.

WOODS are the longest clubs in your bag. They have the longest shaft and are capable of hitting the golf ball farther than any of the other golf clubs. Woods also have the biggest hitting surface of any club. The clubheads are shaped like half moons. Woods are used for distance and direction and are often used for a golfer's first shot (tee shot) on a golf hole. When you hit with a wood you want the ball to travel far and straight. It's always fun to hit with woods because of their ability to hit the ball far down the fairway. Yet woods are one of the most difficult clubs to golf with. The longer shaft makes it more difficult to control, and the shape of the club face makes it easier to hit your golf ball off line. This is due to the **loft** of the club.

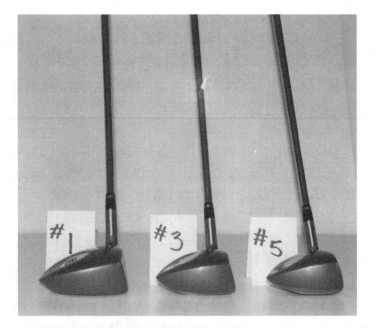

Here is a photo of three clubs: a #1, a #3 and a #5 wood.

LOFT is a very important part of why each golf club hits the way it does. If you set a golf club on the ground you will notice that the top of the clubhead will be tilted away from the bottom of the clubhead that is resting on the ground. **The amount of tilt you see between the top and bottom of the clubhead is the club's loft.**

The amount of loft in a clubhead controls how high the ball travels. The more loft you see in a clubhead, the higher in the air the ball will travel. For instance, put a #1 wood and a #5 wood on the ground next to each other. You will clearly see that the #5 wood has more tilt or loft between the top and bottom of the clubhead than the #1 wood. This means the #5 wood will send the ball higher in the air than the #1 wood but not as far down the fairway. The higher a ball goes, the less distance it will cover. So you would use a #1 wood if you had to hit the ball a great distance. If you still wanted to hit your ball with the distance of a wood but wanted the ball to go higher in the air when you hit it, you would use the #5 wood. Remember that a #5 wood does not go as far as a #1 wood.

Now look at a #3 iron and a #9 iron side by side touching the ground. Again you can see that the #9 iron has much more loft than the #3 iron. What does this mean about each club's ability to hit the ball? Of course it means that the #3 iron will hit the ball far but not very high and the #9 iron will hit the ball very high but not very far. If you were in a situation to hit a shot with an iron and wanted lots of distance and not much height, you would choose to hit with the #3 iron. If you were close to the green and wanted to hit the ball high, but not very far, the #9 iron would be a great choice.

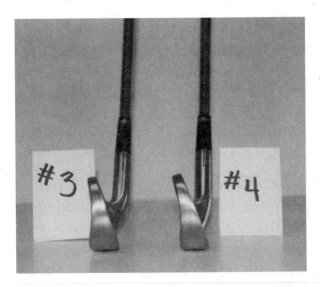

Left: This is a photo of the long irons: the #3 and #4 irons. These will hit the ball long but not to high.

Right: This is a photo of the mid-irons: the #5, #6 and #7 irons. Notice the difference in the loft or tilt of these clubs.

Remember also that the higher the ball goes, the less it will roll once it hits the ground. This is another good reason to use a golf club with lots of loft as you get close to the green. If you hit your shot to the green and it lands with little to no roll, your shot will end up on the green where you planned. And remember, irons are often easier to control than woods because of their shorter shaft.

TIGER SAYS

Here's an easy way to remember what each club does - the higher the number of the club, the higher the golf ball will travel (but less distance) . . . the lower the number of the club, the lower the ball will travel (with more distance).

Take a look at one of your irons and you will notice narrow grooves that run across the clubface. These grooves are designed to make the golf ball spin backwards when you hit it. This is called putting backspin on the ball. Backspin does several things. When a ball with backspin lands on the ground, it tends to stop where it lands rather than continuing to roll. Backspin also helps the ball travel high and straight down the fairway towards the hole when you hit it.

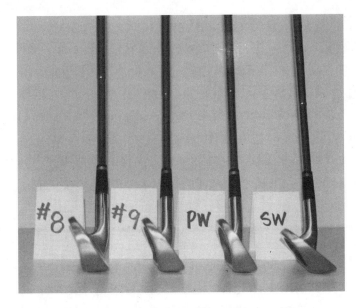

Left: This is a picture of the short irons: #8 & #9 irons. Also the Pitching Wedge and Sand Wedge are shown. Notice the difference in each club's tilt.

The **PITCHING WEDGE** is another important golf club. Pitching wedges have a lot of loft in their clubface. Remember this loft makes their shots go very high without covering a great deal of distance. You often will use the pitching wedge when you are approaching the green and have less than 100 yards to hit the ball. Because of the club's ability to hit the ball very high, a pitching wedge is useful when a player needs to hit their ball high in the air over trees, water or sand. The loft of the pitching wedge also helps the golfer hit out of tall grass or rough that surrounds the fairway on a golf hole. Because of the amount of loft, this club tends to give the ball a great deal of backspin so it stays where it lands on the green without rolling one way or the other.

Hitting out of a bunker is like hitting your ball at the beach. That's why we have a **SAND WEDGE**. The sand wedge, like the pitching wedge, has a great deal of loft to get the ball up and out of the sand. The club also has a very wide and flat bottom called the flange. The flange of the club allows it to slide easily through the sand and under the ball, making it easier to lift your ball out of the bunker.

Once you have reached the green or gotten very close to the green, you will use your **PUTTER** to roll the ball into the hole. Look at your putter. You will notice that the clubface has very little loft at all. In fact the clubface is almost straight up and down. This is because the putter does not lift the ball like the other golf clubs. The putter simply strokes the ball and rolls it into the hole. When you hit the ball with the putter you want it to travel as smoothly across the green as possible. Putting may be the most important part of a golfer's game.

TIGER SAYS

If you are a good putter you can often make up for any bad shots you may have had approaching the hole.

The goal of putting is not always to put the ball into the hole, but rather close to the hole. If you can putt the ball close enough to the hole on your first putt of any green and sink it on the second putt, it will help your golf score a great deal.

When hitting with your woods or irons, you always want to hit with the center of the clubface called the "sweetspot."

TIGER SAYS

Hitting the ball with the center of your clubface, or "sweetspot", will help the ball travel straight towards the hole. This "sweetspot" of the clubface also gives the ball the most backspin as it travels.

Hitting the ball off the clubface can have different effects.

- **SLICE:** If the ball is hit with the toe of the club behind the heel, with an outside-in swing path, the ball will spin from left to right. This means a right-handed golfer will curve the ball to the right and a left-handed golfer will curve the ball to the left. This shot is called a SLICE.

- **HOOK**: If the ball is hit with the the toe of the club in front of the heel, with an inside-out swing path, the ball will spin from right to left. This means a right-handed golfer will curve the ball to the left and a left-handed golfer will curve the ball to the right. This shot is called a HOOK.

When you hit any wood or iron shot with the center of the clubface, it will travel the straightest and the farthest towards the hole. Hitting with the sweetspot of each club also will give your shot the best backspin so your ball stops where it lands.

As you begin to hit with the different golf clubs, you will get a good idea of how far you can hit each club. When you begin to play on an actual golf course, it will help a great deal to have a good idea what club to use in any situation on the course. There is a rule of thumb as to how far each club will hit when comparing irons with irons and woods with woods. A simple rule for comparing clubs is:

- Each numbered iron, starting from the low numbered irons, will hit 10 yards further than the higher numbered iron. This means the #3 iron will hit 10 yards farther than the #4 iron and the #4 iron will hit 10 yards farther than the #5 iron and so on.

- Each numbered wood, starting from the low numbered woods, will hit 15 yards further than the higher numbered wood. This means the #1 wood will hit 15 yards farther than the #2 wood and the #2 wood will hit 15 yards farther than the #3 wood and so on.

TIGER SAYS

Once you have hit with most of the golf clubs in your bag on the driving range, you will have a feel for how far you can hit each club. Then you can use the yard difference above to help you determine the best club to use for your shots on the golf course.

Know how far you can hit each club.

Now that you have some ideas on what club could be used in any golfing situation, let's join Tiger out on the golf course and help our friend pick the best club for each shot. Remember some of the questions may have more than one answer since you often can use several clubs in any golfing situation. The answers appear at the end of this chapter.

1. Tiger is ready to begin his golf game on the first hole of the golf course. Tiger's scorecard shows the distance from the tee to the hole is 320 yards. Tiger wants to hit the ball far without sending it too high in the air. What club should Tiger use to hit this shot?

2. Poor Tiger! Our friend has popped up the tee shot and it only traveled 120 yards. The shot is in the middle of the fairway but is still 200 yards from the hole. If Tiger usually hits a #1 wood 230 yards, what club would you give Tiger to use to hit this shot?

3. Tiger can usually hit the #5 iron 130 yards. Tiger's ball now sits 100 yards from the green. Tiger has a straight approach to the green and does not need to hit the ball over any trees or water. Tiger thinks the next shot can land on the green and wants the ball to have lots of backspin so it stops where it lands. What might be the best club for Tiger to use to get the next shot close to the hole on the green?

4. On no! Tiger has hit the ball into the bunker right next to the green. It is not too far from the hole but Tiger will have to use a club that will get his ball out of the bunker. What club can you give Tiger to help save the score on this hole?

5. Tiger has hit a great shot out of the bunker but has gone over the green and the ball is sitting on the fringe of the green, the narrow area of short grass that lies between the fairway and the green. Tiger is about 20 feet from the hole. There are several clubs Tiger could use to get the ball close to the hole. But Tiger is much better with the short irons (chipping) than with the putter from off the green. With this in mind what club might you suggest Tiger use to successfully get the ball close to the hole?

6. Since you've done such a good job of helping Tiger with this hole we'll make this last question really, really easy. Tiger has hit the shot onto the green and is only 6 feet from the hole (finally!). What club would you give Tiger from the golf bag to finish this hole up?

ANSWERS TO TIGER'S GOLFING QUESTIONS

1. Tiger will need to hit his driver (#1 wood) or a #3 wood.

2. Tiger could use a #3 wood.

3. Tiger would use a #8 iron to hit this shot. Since there is a 10 yard difference between each of the irons and Tiger can hit a #5 iron 130 yards, a #8 iron would be the right club to use
   #5 iron = 130 yards
   #6 iron = 120 yards
   #7 iron = 110 yards
   #8 iron = 100 yards

4. Tiger would use a sand wedge to hit out of the bunker.

5. Since Tiger hits well with short irons, Tiger may want to hit this chip shot onto the green with a #7 iron (look up the definition for chip shot in the "Golf Terms" chapter if you have forgotten what it means!).

6. Here, of course, Tiger would use a putter!

CHAPTER 4
Getting Started

By this point you've learned about the terms used in golf and you've read about balls, clubs, scorecards and golf holes. You've also learned about how a golf club works. Now you're ready to get started!

There are three items you'll need to get started playing the game of golf:
- Golf Clubs
- A Golf Bag with Balls and Tees
- Golf Shoes or Tennis Shoes and Proper Clothing

GOLF CLUBS

When you begin to play golf, it is best to borrow or rent your golf clubs. This way you can try a variety of types of clubs and get a feeling for what brand feels right and hits your golf ball the best. Borrow or share some clubs with a friend who golfs or rent them when you go to the golf course to play. Also be sure to ask the golf professional at the golf course what clubs they feel might work best for a person of your size and ability. The golf professional is there to help people who play on their golf course and often has advice and ideas for beginning golfers. When you are considering what clubs to use, a golf professional can provide valuable advice on the weight of the clubs you should use, the thickness and type of grip for your hand size and what brand might work best for a person with your experience. Some Junior Golf Programs will give you a free club when you sign up for lessons – check with your golf facility.

A beginner's set of golf clubs would most likely contain the following clubs:
- A #1 Wood (Driver) or a #3 Wood
- A #3 Iron, a #5 Iron, a #7 Iron and a #9 Iron
- A Pitching Wedge
- A Putter

Wait until you have played golf for some time before purchasing your own set of clubs. By borrowing, sharing and renting clubs, you will get a good idea of what works best for you. And if you are still growing, you may want to carefully consider when the best time to purchase clubs will be. A child can easily outgrow a set of golf clubs during a growth spurt so plan carefully when buying your own clubs.

A GOLF BAG

You will, of course, need a golf bag to carry your clubs around the golf course. Most rental clubs will come with a bag, as will any clubs that you might borrow.

A golf bag does not need to be very fancy. A plastic bag with leather supports and a pocket will work great. Your golf balls and tees can go in the bag's pocket. Also, you may want to keep a few extra pencils and a golf rule book in this pocket.

Be sure to keep enough balls in the bag's pocket to replace any you might lose while playing golf. There are a lot of places on a course that a ball can get lost and you don't want to be on a golf hole far away from the golf shop and run out of balls. Take more than you think you'll need. That way you'll have enough for you and any friends you may be golfing with.

You may want to use a different color or brand name of ball than the people you golf with. This will make it easy to find your ball and hit your next shot. Used balls are also a good and inexpensive idea for beginning golfers. Beginners may lose lots of balls when they first start golfing and used balls are very inexpensive.

Also be sure to have at least 20 tees in your bag. Tees can easily get broken or lost on every golf hole when you hit your tee shot. Be sure you have a new tee for each of the 18 golf holes on the course (plus a few extras!).

Before you tee off, make sure you have enough golf balls and tees to finish playing the golf course.

GOLF SHOES & PROPER CLOTHING

The proper shoes for golf are an important part of getting started. Golf shoes have short steel or plastic spikes on the bottom of the shoes and keep a golfer from slipping when they are hitting their shots. While golf shoes are your best choice to wear when you are playing golf, sneakers also will work. Be sure to wear a pair of sneakers that are not too worn on the bottom so they will give you a good grip on the ground when you swing.

Also, be sure to dress appropriately for the golf course you are playing at. It is best to check with the golf professional about the "Dress Code" of the course. One golf course may say t-shirts are okay to play golf in while another may require collared shirts. Different golf courses have different dress codes and it is best for you and your friends to be properly dressed when you arrive to play golf. Also be sure the clothing you wear for golf is comfortable and loose fitting. Tight clothing will restrict your movement and make it more difficult to swing and hit the ball. Loose clothing does not restrict your movement and makes swinging a golf club much easier.

You also may want to wear a golf glove when you play golf. Beginners often will get blisters on their hands from holding too tight while swinging clubs. A golf glove will not only help stop these blisters, but also will give you a better grip on the golf club.

When you call to make your tee time, ask about the dress code of the golf course.

SWING CLINIC AND LESSONS

Before you head out onto a golf course to play a real round of golf, it is a good idea to take some golf lessons or attend a swing clinic.

A golf instructor helps students in a beginning swing clinic.

TIGER SAYS

There are a number of places to take golf lessons. Golf courses, driving ranges, most city recreation departments, YMCAs and even some schools will offer golf lessons.

Books, magazines and video programs are a good way to get more information on how to swing a golf club. There are even junior golf camps that will teach golfers how to golf well. Also, most local golf courses will have a Junior Golf Program. Ask the golf professional at your course about junior golf programs in your area. Many professionals offer regular swing clinics for groups of golfers and most professionals give individual lessons.

Check the bulletin board at your nearest golf course or driving range to find out about upcoming swing clinics.

Regardless of where you take your lessons, be sure to get professional instruction on your golf swing before you attempt your first round of golf on the course.

When you are in your lesson or swing clinic, be sure to pay close attention to your instructor or golf professional. This professional will give you tips when you are first starting to play golf that will help you develop a great golf swing. Pay close

This golf professional is helping Jessica perfect her form during a swing clinic.

The instructor explains how to use "The Rules of Golf" book.

attention to the rules and regulations of golf your instructor will cover as these are as important to your game as your swing. We'll cover golf rules and golfing etiquette in later chapters.

If you have a parent or relative that enjoys the game of golf you may want to ask them to go with you to the course and hit some balls on the driving range. If they are experienced golfers with a good swing they can watch you hit balls and give you helpful hints on improving your swing.

PRACTICE

You can never practice too much before you go out and play your first round of golf. This is such an important point the we're going to say it one more time.

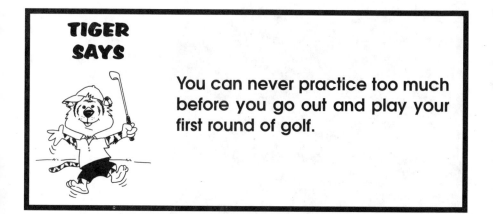

With the increase in the popularity of golf, most golf courses and many neighborhoods have driving ranges where golfers can practice hitting golf balls. Many of these ranges also have lights so golfers can practice their golf game after the sun has gone down. For a few dollars at the range, a golfer can buy a bucket of balls that belongs to the driving range and hit the balls out into the range's large "fairway." This "fairway" often will have signs marking the distance the balls are being hit and also will have golf flags sticking up at different distances like real golf holes. This way a golfer, who is working on their swing, can practice both accuracy and distance.

Marcie is practicing her irons.

Young golfers practice their chipping form.

For the beginning golfer the driving range is a great place to work on their swing. Before you play your first round of golf you should know how far you can hit each golf club. Practicing at the driving range will give you a good idea how far the ball will go with each different club. By determining this at the range you will know what clubs to use in any situation when you are playing on a real course.

TIGER SAYS

Hit enough practice balls at the driving range before you play on a real golf course to determine how far you can hit each golf club.

Most ranges also have a practice putting green for visiting golfers to use. Here golfers use their own balls and practice their putting by rolling their ball into a number of different holes on the practice green. The grass on the practice putting green is cut and maintained much like the grass on an actual golf course green. Also many practice greens have a small fringe of grass around the edge for golfers to practice putting from.

Junior golfers take turns practicing their putting.

TIGER SAYS

Go to the practice putting green with a friend and take turns putting into each of the holes. Keep track of how many strokes it takes each of you to get the ball into the hole.

Some ranges also have a small bunker near the putting green for golfers to practice hitting their bunker shots. All these opportunities to practice your golf shots before you head out to the course mean one thing . . . You can never practice too much before you go out and play your first round of golf!

READY TO PLAY GOLF . . .

After you have taken several golf lessons or been to a swing clinic and spent time hitting balls on the driving range and on the practice putting green, you probably are ready to play a round of golf!

Ask the golf professional or your golf instructor you've been working with when they think you are ready to play on a golf course. And also ask that person where they recommend you play your first round of golf. Golf courses are all very different. Some courses are very expensive and

Begin playing on an executive or short golf course.

difficult to play, while others may be less expensive and designed more for a less advanced golfer. Municipal and public courses are often the best place for a new golfer to play their first round of golf. An executive course is also a good place for beginners to start because the holes are shorter and less difficult than regulation golf courses. Often times public courses are designed for the average golfer and many encourage junior golfers to play. Some courses have age limits for players and may require younger golfers to golf with an adult in their group. If this is the case, ask your parents or a relative who likes to golf to join you for a round or golf.

You probably will want to make a tee time at the course you are going to play. If you are at the course simply go into the golf shop and ask them for a tee time on a specific day. You will need to know what day you want to play, how many people will be playing with you and what name the tee time should be listed under. If you do not live close to the actual course, you can call the golf shop on the telephone and ask for a tee time. Telephone numbers for most golf courses can be found in the telephone directory yellow pages. When you have arranged a day and a time to play golf (tee time), be sure you and your group arrive 15 to 20 minutes before your tee time. When you get to the course, check in with the golf shop and let them know you and your group have arrived. The person in the golf shop will note your arrival and call out the name of your group when it is your turn to tee off.

Show up at least 15 to 20 minutes before your tee time.

As we mentioned before, be sure you and your group are properly dressed for the golf course you are playing. It is a good idea to ask about the course's dress code when you call for your tee time. Also make sure you have enough balls and tees in your bag to last you for a round of golf. Get some pencils and a scorecard from the golf shop while you are waiting for your tee time. While you and your group are waiting for your tee time, always review the course rules that often are written on the back of the scorecard.

Kelsie and Evan read the rules on the back of the scorecard before they tee off.

While you are waiting for your tee time you also should do several minutes of warm-up stretching. Swinging a golf club uses many of your body's muscles and your body should be warmed up and loose before you swing your clubs. This will help to avoid any sprains, pulled muscles or injuries while you are golfing.

One popular warm-up stretch is to put a club behind your back and between your elbows. With your feet shoulder length apart slowly turn your body to the right and then to the left. Only

Be sure to warm up properly before hitting balls on the range or on the course.

turn as far as is comfortable and never turn far enough to a point where the stretch hurts your body.

For another excellent stretch, hold the golf club in front of your waist and bend from your waist towards the ground. Only bend down to a point where it does not hurt your body and hold your stretch when you bend (do not bounce). Do both these stretches before you hit your tee shot and your body and muscles will be well warmed up.

Soon you and your golfing friends will hear your name announced as next up on the first tee. It's the moment you and your friends have been waiting for as you step up to your first golf hole and tee up your ball!

TIGER'S EXTRA TIPS

If you can't make it to the golf course or driving range, there are several fun ways to practice golf at home with a friend.

You can practice your putting on some short carpet at home. Set up a small plastic glass that is close to the size of a golf hole and use it as a target as you putt balls from different directions and distances towards the cup.

Another great way to practice your chip shots at home is to find a patch of lawn that is okay to be cut up with a golf club (ask your parents). Buy an old umbrella from a second hand store and place the open umbrella 10 to 15 yards away from you and a friend. With your pitching wedge practice hitting balls up into the air and into the open umbrella.

TIGER SAYS

The two most important parts of any golfer's game is their short game and their putting. Practicing these two areas in your golf game can do more to save you strokes and give you a better golf game than practicing with any other clubs.

CHAPTER 5
The Golf Swing

There is only one way to develop a good golf swing. Like throwing a baseball, catching a football or shooting a basket, the only way to learn and get better at each of these sports is to just do it! Golf is not different. An effective golf swing can be learned only with proper instruction and practice. A book cannot help you perfect your golf swing. Only practice and instruction from a professional can do that. What a book can do is provide tips and ideas for you to think about each time you swing a golf club.

And that's what this chapter will do. Creating a great golf swing will happen on the course and at the driving range with lots of practice and playing. This chapter will give you some general ideas and tips to think about to help make your golf swing the best it can be.

GOLF SWING FUNDAMENTALS

To swing a golf club correctly always keep in mind the three fundamentals of a good golf swing:

- The **GRIP**
- The **SET-UP**
- The **ALIGNMENT**

The **GRIP** refers to how you place your hands on the handle of the golf club. Your grip affects the direction that the club face meets the ball.

The following three pictures show the three most common ways to grip the golf club:

Left: This is a photo of the 10 finger grip. Make sure all 10 fingers are on the golf club.

Left: This is a photo of the interlock grip. The little finger of the right hand is interlocked with the index finger of the left hand. (opposite for left-handed golfers)

Right: This is a photo of the overlap grip. The little finger of the right hand is overlapped on the index finger of the left hand. (opposite for left-handed golfers)

The **SET-UP** refers to your posture or body position over the ball when you address (approach) it. Your set-up affects the path that your golf club swings.

Bend from the waist

Arms hanging straight down

slight knee bend

Kelsie stands nice and tall with a slight bend at her waist and her knees slightly bent.

ALIGNMENT is how you aim your club and body to the target. Your alignment to the target affects where your ball will land after you hit it.

Left: Line up your clubhead to the target . . .

Right: Then line up your body. The clubhead is aimed at the target while the body is aimed parallel to the left of the target.

All three of these factors; **GRIP, SET-UP** and **ALIGNMENT** will determine where your ball will fly and land.

There are five basic parts of a golf swing:

- The **TAKEAWAY** where the club begins moving away from the ball.

- The **BACKSWING** where the club comes up and away from the ball.

- The **DOWNSWING** where the club comes down toward the ball.

- The **POINT OF IMPACT** where the club face strikes the ball.

- The **FOLLOW-THROUGH** where the club continues through the swing to end up in the correct finishing position.

GENERAL GOLF SWING TIPS

There are a number of general tips to keep in mind when you swing a golf club:

- Like any other sport you should stretch your muscles before you practice your swing. This will not only loosen up your body and give you more control over your swing but also will help reduce the risk of injury.

- The golf swing has the same motion as throwing a ball or swinging a bat - the movement of the golf swing goes from your back foot to your front foot.

- Try to think of swinging the golf club when you swing and try not to think of hitting the ball.

Swing with the "flow" of the golf club.

- Be sure to stay relaxed during your golf swing - if you become tight during your swing, it will not be smooth and it will be difficult to keep your balance.

- Always keep your chin pointing at the ball during your swing - this will help you make solid contact with the ball.

Kelsie's chin is pointed toward the ball during her swing.

- Your head should not move up or down and your body should not straighten up until you have swung the club through the golf ball.

- **Stance** - for the longer clubs (woods and longer irons), your feet should be as wide apart as your shoulders. For shorter irons, your feet should be slightly closer together than your shoulder width. These stances will help you keep your balance.

Below: Jessica's feet are shoulder width apart for her woods.

Above: Jessica uses a narrower stance for iron shots.

SPECIFIC GOLF SWING TIPS

1. Your **TAKEAWAY** should start close to the ground and your **BACKSWING** should finish with your hands above your shoulder and your back facing the target.

2. At the top of your **BACKSWING** most of your weight should be on your right foot with your hips and shoulders turned to the right.

Your back to the target

Weight on your right side

This is the top of Kelsie's backswing.

3. When you get the club to the top of your **BACKSWING**, you should have a short pause before you begin your **DOWNSWING**.

4. On the **DOWNSWING**, bring your body weight from your right leg to your left leg by turning your hips towards the target. This should bring the club to the ball on the same path that it went up on.

5. Try to swing the club through the bottom of the ball at the **POINT OF IMPACT** to make the ball go up in the air - keeping your knees bent throughout your swing will decrease the chance of hitting the top of your golf ball.

Swing through the ball.

6. At the finish of your swing, or your **FOLLOW-THROUGH** you should be facing your target with your weight on your left leg and your hands by your left ear.

At the finish of Kelsie's swing, her weight is on her left leg, with her body facing her target, and her hands are up by her ear.

TROUBLESHOOTING YOUR GOLF SWING

1. If you hit lots of grass and make a divot behind your ball, your weight may be on your back foot rather than your front foot during your downswing. As you begin your downswing, be sure to shift your weight to your front foot.

2. If you are not making solid contact with the ball, your head may be popping up or down or moving from side to side. This causes your clubface not to meet the ball in its sweetspot. Keep your eyes on the ball and your chin pointed towards your ball throughout your swing to make solid contact between the clubface and the ball. Your head comes up in your follow through.

3. If your ball flies straight right or straight left, it may mean your hands are pointing the clubface in either of those directions at the point of impact. If this happens check that your grip on the club is correct.

4. If your ball curves to the right or to the left, it may mean that the path you are swinging your club is incorrect. If you are having this problem check your set-up and your alignment to the target.

5. If you keep hitting the top of your golf ball and your shots do not get up in the air, check your knees. They should remain bent throughout your swing.

FINAL THOUGHTS ON YOUR GOLF SWING

Keep these swing tips in mind as you work on developing a strong and solid golf swing. The tips we covered will give you a solid foundation for working on your swing.

TIGER SAYS

The best way to create a good swing is to take lessons or attend a swing clinic. And then practice . . . practice . . . practice. Like any sport getting out and doing it is the best way to work on your technique and fix any problems or inconsistencies you may have. As you spend more time practicing on the driving range, you will see your shots getting better, you will feel more control over all your clubs and all the shots you hit. Patience and practice are the two main ingredients in developing a great golf swing.

CHAPTER 6
Golf Rules & Safety

Like any sport, golf has it's own set of rules to follow. But unlike many other sports that use an umpire or a referee to make sure rules are followed, golf is played on the honor system. This means it is up to each player to follow the rules of the game and also up to each player to be familiar with the rules of golf.

Each golfer keeps track of their own score while playing a round of golf. Therefore it is up to you, and the other golfers in your group, to keep track of all your strokes on each hole and record them on your scorecard after you have finished each hole. Strokes are added to your score when you lose balls or land in specific areas of the golf course. It is important that you know when to add strokes to your game and be familiar with what is considered a penalty situation and what is not.

This chapter will cover some of the most common rules of the game of golf so a beginning golfer can be familiar with them and follow them on their very first round of golf. This chapter also will cover golfing safety, another very important part of being a golfer and golfing with others on a golf course.

TIGER SAYS Know all the rules of the game of golf. They have been created to help you play and understand golf better. Not following the rules doesn't help a player's golf game in any way.

1. You may carry up to, but not more than, 14 clubs in your golf bag. There is a two stroke penalty added to your score if you break this rule.

2. Count all your strokes until your golf ball is in the hole. This includes all penalty strokes and times you may have missed the ball while swinging (called a "whiff").

Count all your strokes.

3. You always must play your ball where it lies, and you cannot touch your golf ball until you reach the green of the hole you are playing. Once on the green, your ball may be cleaned and marked. The only reason to touch your ball while playing down the fairway would be if you had to reposition your ball in a penalty or free drop situation.

Left: Play it where it lies... "good".

Right: Play it where it lies... "bad".

Left: Play it where it lies... "ugly".

Josh shows that you can tee your ball up no more than two club lengths behind the tee markers on the tee box.

4. The teeing ground at each hole is an imaginary square that runs two club lengths behind the tee markers. This is the area from which a golfer must hit their tee shot. If you are outside of these boundaries you must take a two stroke penalty and must tee off again.

5. If your ball falls off the tee before your downswing or at your address (before you even begin your backswing), you may tee up your ball again without taking a penalty stroke.

If your ball falls off the tee during your downswing... sorry it's a stroke.

6. When you hit your ball into a golf hazard (bunker, water, etc.) you cannot ground your club in that hazard at address. This means your club cannot touch the ground until you hit your shot from the hazard. If you do touch the ground you must add one penalty stroke to your score.

Do not ground your club in a golf hazard.

7. You have five minutes to look for a lost ball. If you have not found your ball in five minutes you must play your provisional ball or put a new ball in play.

You have five minutes to look for a lost ball!

TIGER SAYS

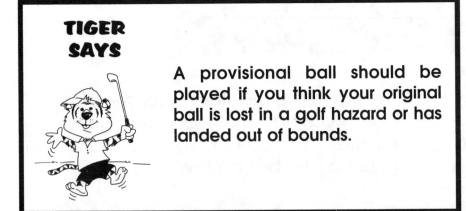

A provisional ball should be played if you think your original ball is lost in a golf hazard or has landed out of bounds.

8. If your ball goes into a water hazard, you must take one penalty stroke and drop a new ball in play or retrieve your original ball. This ball is dropped two club lengths from where your ball entered the water and cannot be closer to the hole.

9. If your ball is too close to a tree, other natural hazard or an artificial object to hit it, you may take one penalty stroke and move your ball away from the tree or obstruction. Your ball must be dropped two club lengths away from the tree or obstruction without placing it closer to the hole than your original shot.

10. If your ball is lost or out-of-bounds, you must add one penalty stroke to your score and play from where you last hit your shot.

11. A player cannot touch their line of putt to the hole except to pick up a loose twig, rock or leaf or to repair a ball mark. There is a two stroke penalty for touching your line of putt.

12. You are finished on each golf hole when your ball is resting in the cup. There is a two stroke penalty if you do not finish a golf hole.

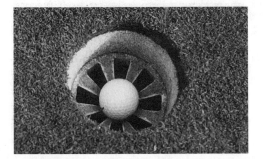

This ball is "holed out."

GENERAL GOLF SAFETY

Since golf most often is played in groups, it is very important to be careful when golfing and to play the game safely. There are a few general safety rules that should be followed to insure that everyone that you golf with plays the game safely.

    1. Always stand behind the person hitting the ball. NEVER stand in front of them. This will lessen the chance of anyone getting hit with a golf ball.

Stay behind any golfer to avoid being hit by the club or ball.

Always look around before you swing.

2. Always look all around before swinging any golf club. Make sure there is no one close enough to you that could get hit by the club or the ball.

3. There never should be any horseplay, fighting or wrestling while on the golf course. Always pay attention to your golf game, as well as the games of everyone in your golfing group.

4. The golfing group in front of you should be well out of your way before you hit your next shot. Never hit your ball if there is any chance of hitting the group in front of you.

5. If your ball is heading in the direction of any other players yell "FORE." Yelling "FORE" is common courtesy to warn other golfers that a ball may be coming in their direction.

Always yell "Fore" if your ball is heading towards anyone.

6. Do not hit your shots to the green until the group ahead of you has finished the hole and left the green. Never hit your approach shot until the golfers ahead of you are safely off the green.

Jodi waits for Marcie and Kelsie to leave the green before she swings.

7. Never lose your temper on the golf course and NEVER throw a golf club anywhere or anytime. Throwing a golf club on a golf course could get you thrown off that course and perhaps suspended from ever golfing at that course again. If you hit a

bad shot or do poorly on a hole, control your temper and think about what you could do on the next hole to do better. **That's one of the great things about golf . . . each hole offers a new opportunity for an excellent score.**

Never throw a golf club in anger.

If your ball lands in another group's fairway let them play first.

Josh and Taylor look over some golf rules.

A good golfer knows the rules of the game and follows them. A good golfer also practices a safe game of golf for themselves and those around them. Following the rules and safety tips outlined in this chapter will allow you to play the game correctly and safety. To receive a booklet covering the complete rules of golf you can write to:

United States Golf Association
Liberty Corner Road
Far Hills, NJ 07931

CHAPTER 7
Golf Etiquette

Over the years of the game, golf has developed its own "unwritten" rules of play called etiquette. Golf etiquette is a set of guidelines that should be followed by every golfer. Where most rules address your actions while playing the game, golf etiquette is based on how your treat other golfers on the course, the people in your golf group and the golf course itself.

An easy way to practice good etiquette is to treat other players on the course the way you would like to be treated. By doing this you will be practicing good golf etiquette.

The information in this chapter will provide an overview of etiquette on the golf course so you will know how to act and what to do from your first day on the golf course.

GENERAL GOLF ETIQUETTE

1. Be familiar with the specific rules of the golf course you are playing. Be sure to check on the dress code and any special rules that apply to young and beginning golfers.

2. Groups of golfers should not have more than four players. This is called a foursome. If there are more than four players in your golfing group you must split into more than one group and play the course separately.

3. Always report to the golf shop when you arrive for your tee time. You should arrive 15-20 minutes before your time. This way the person in the golf shop knows your group is ready to golf and will announce your group's name when your tee time arrives.

4. Practice "ready" golf. This means always be ready when it is your turn to hit. Understand the rules of who hits first in a golf group and always be aware of when your turn is coming up. Also try to use only one practice swing before you hit your shot. While there is no time limit in golf it is important to keep your group moving so other players can continue to play.

5. Be considerate of all other players on the golf course. This means to keep your voice down and try not to move around anymore than is necessary when others are playing their shots. Shouting and running around are not permitted on a golf course.

Do not run around and be loud on the golf course.

6. As we mentioned in the previous chapter on safety, always wait until the group in front of you is off the green or far enough away that your shot will not reach them before you hit your shots.

7. Always try to go golfing with a friend and share the fun. And always walk the course no matter what your age. As well as being a great sport, golf can be a great way to exercise and stay healthy.

Evan, Marcie, Kelsie and Jodi
enjoy a round of golf together.

8. Always leave the golf course in better condition than when you arrived. This means not only taking care of the course itself, but also throwing away all your trash at the end of your round.

Leave the golf course in better condition than when you got there.

9. You and your golfing partners should not use any bad or obscene language any time you play golf. Sportsmanship and controlling your temper are very important parts of playing golf.

GOLF ETIQUETTE ON THE FAIRWAY

1. The player with the lowest score on the previous hole always hits first on the tee of the next hole. If two or more players had the same score on the last hole you would go to the scores of the previous hole until one of the golfer's score was lower than the others. On the first hole of the golfing round it is up to the group who hits the first tee shot.

2. Always be quiet and still when other golfers in your group are hitting their shots. This goes for putting, as well as fairway and tee shots.

3. Help your golfing partners by watching where their golf ball goes after they hit it. This can save a great deal of time and result in a lot less lost balls and penalty strokes!

Rather than talking to each other (as shown above) . . .
watch and follow your playing partner's ball when they
hit (as shown below).

4. Use landmarks on the course to keep track of where your ball lands, as well as the balls of other members in your group. This will make it easier to find your ball or another player's ball for the next shot.

5. If you or someone else in your group is looking for a ball, let the groups behind you play through. And if you cannot find a lost ball in five minutes consider it a lost ball, take the penalty stroke or strokes and play your provisional ball.

Water Hazards - Leave your ball in the water, don't go swimming after it.

6. If your ball goes deep into a water hazard where it will be difficult to get out, do not go in "swimming" after your ball. Consider it a lost ball, take your penalty strokes and play a another ball or your provisional ball.

7. Always replace your divots on the fairway right away. Doing this keeps the golf course looking nice and may stop another player's ball from landing in the hole the divot made.

Always replace your divots RIGHT AWAY.

8. Always rake the sand in the bunker after you have hit your ball out. Be sure to rake over the area where you hit your shot as well as any footprints that may be in the bunker.

Evan rakes the bunker after hitting his ball out of the sand.

GOLF ETIQUETTE ON THE GREEN

1. Pick up your feet when you walk on the green. This keeps the grass on the green nice and smooth, making it easier to putt on.

Pick up your feet when you walk on the green.

*On the green, try to fix your
ball mark plus two others.*

2. When you fix the ball mark on the green where your ball has landed, take the time to fix at least two other ball marks. Doing this will help the green look its best.

3. When you and your group reach the green, be careful not to step in any other player's line of putting. This means avoid stepping on the grass that their ball will have to travel over when they putt their ball into the hole.

Avoid stepping in another player's line of putting. This photograph shows bad etiquette.

4. If your ball is in the way of another players putt who is further away from the hole, you must mark your ball's position on the green. Mark it with a ball marker or coin and pick-up your ball until the other player has stroked their putt. Once they have taken their shot, you can replace your ball and take your turn. Other than relief situations (ground under repair, casual water, etc.), this is the only time you can touch your ball without a penalty stroke.

5. The player farthest from the hole putts first on the green. This order (farthest from the hole putts first) continues, until all balls are in the hole. However, to help with faster play, a person may continue to hit their ball until it is in the hole.

6. Always set your golf bag down, off of the green, closest to the next hole. Placing your golf bag full of clubs on the green will damage the grass.

Leave your bag to the side of the green towards the next hole.

7. When you and your group are finished on the green, move on to the next hole to record your scores. This will allow the group behind you to continue playing the hole.

Left: Do not record your scores on the green.

Right: Move on to the next hole and then mark your scorecard.

LET'S GO PLAY GOLF!

Above all remember that golf is supposed to be fun. It gives you a great opportunity to play an enjoyable game that you can play for the rest of your life. It also is a great activity to share with friends and family members who enjoy an afternoon on the golf course. And it is a fun and exciting way to get plenty of exercise and enjoy the outdoors.

We hope you enjoyed *Tiger's Tips*. By practicing and following the information in this book you will have a better understanding of the game and the information you need to hit your first tee shot on a real golf course.

TIGER SAYS

Remember the key to becoming a good golfer is to be patient and practice . . . practice . . . and practice some more. And the most important part of playing golf is to always have a great time.

So have fun and keep golfing!

A VERY SPECIAL THANKS TO:

The Tiger's Tips Kids
and
The Staff at the
Oceanside Municipal
Golf Course

Please write Tiger at:
TigersTips@aol.com
or
Tiger's Tips
P.O. Box 1852
Carlsbad, CA 92018

Index

About The Authors

Donald J. Emerick

Having grown up in Junior Golf in Ohio, Don Emerick's entire life has been devoted to the game of golf and the values the game brings with it. He has been playing since he was ten years old and has worked at a golf course since he was thirteen. In 1989, he was named Assistant Professional of the Year by the San Diego Chapter of the PGA, he is a member of the PGA and a golf instructor in Oceanside, California. The entire Emerick family, including his wife Terrie and daughter Kelsie, play golf and enjoy the time they spend on the golf course.

Ken Kebow

Producer/director Ken Kebow has been creating educational and entertaining video programs for over ten years. Kebow has produced programs for numerous large corporations including American Airlines, Prudential Securities and Nissan Motors, as well as for golf companies Taylor Made and Callaway Golf. Also, Kebow independently produced "Blast Off!," an introduction for kids to America's space program which currently is being distributed by Hallmark Home Entertainment and was the winner of a 1995 Parent's Choice Award.

Dean Baldridge

As owner of D.B. Designs, Dean Baldridge has been working for the last ten years in the graphic design field. His work includes illustrations, cartoons, logo design, silk screening, layout, magazine and book design. Baldridge has produced work for a number of corporations including Jazzercise, Inc., Wilson Sporting Goods and Tami Lee Webb International (Abs & Buns of Steel fame). For the past five years Baldridge has been teaching art to children in the San Diego School District. Dean and his wife Sally have twin daughters, Marcie and Jodi, who have been in a Junior Golf Program since they were eight years old.

Jim Fisher

Jim Fisher has worked in the golf industry since 1981 starting in the management level with C.C.A. in Southern California. Mr. Fisher has spent time as a national sales manager for a major golf grip company and for the past ten years he has represented some of the biggest golf club manufacturers in the country. Being around the game for so many years and working in the many different aspects of the industry, has given Jim vast knowledge of the tools and mechanics of the game. Jim is a leader in the promotion of Junior Golf and is excited about all the advancements that have been made towards the development of junior education. Having two children has increased Jim's excitement in the junior area with hopes of his children continuing their participation in the game.

A Terrific Book for Young Basketball Players

MAKING THE BASKETBALL TEAM

Get Off The Bench and Into The Game

by Lane Czaplinski

Foreword by Roy Williams

Basketball is an increasingly popular sport - some say the most popular. Yet, as scores of kids compete against their peers for spots and playing time on the team, most come away from the experience feeling completely defeated and perplexed.

Making the Basketball Team will give young men and women the advantage in the very competitive world of basketball. Whether the student-athlete is trying out for their junior high, high school or college team, they will find this book a truly valued asset in making the basketball team.

This book provides a step-by-step approach to making the team and improving skills necessary for realizing one's potential. It gives specific advice on how to approach training for tryouts, concentrating on both physical and mental fundamentals crucial to achieving success on the basketball court.

" *I work with young players every summer and know how tough the competition is for even the really talented athletes. Every young player that is serious about basketball should read this book.*"

– Danny Manning, NBA Forward

Making the Basketball Team is only $7.00 plus $3.00 shipping and handling.

To order, send a check or money order payable to Quality Sports, 24 Buysse Dr., Coal Valley, IL 61240. To conveniently order with Visa, MasterCard or American Express call toll-free **1-800-464-1116**.

Or call 1-800-464-1116 to receive a complimentary brochure on all Quality Sports books.

8 7 6 5